8 D
S_

Learning to defend the Life of Grace

by Vivian Boland, OP

*All booklets are published thanks to the
generous support of the members of the
Catholic Truth Society*

CATHOLIC TRUTH SOCIETY
PUBLISHERS TO THE HOLY SEE

Contents

Introduction

What's in a number?

Three

Certain numbers seem to be more attractive than others in satisfying people's desire for a complete account of something. One of them is the number three. There is a collection of early Celtic wisdom that is presented exclusively in the form of triads. One I remember from school is:

> three slender things that support the world: the stream of milk from the cow, the blade of green corn, the thread over the hand of a skilled woman.

In many of them there is a moral sting in the tail, for example:

> three things that hide: an open bag hides nothing, an open door hides little, an open person hides something.

This kind of popular wisdom is found everywhere, of course. In the Buddhist scriptures, for example, we find two contradictory texts (as often happens with proverbial wisdom) one telling us that the three conditions under which deeds are produced are covetousness, hatred and infatuation, and the other telling us that the conditions under which deeds are produced are freedom from covetousness, freedom from hatred, and freedom from infatuation. An early philosopher, Clinias, denounced the three causes of perverse actions as love of pleasure, greed and love of honour. Not surprisingly we find triadic wisdom also in the Bible. We often chant, without batting an eyelid, that:

> God has said only one thing: only two do I know: that to God alone belongs power and to you, Lord, love; and that you repay each one according to his deeds (*Ps* 62:11-12).

The author of Sirach tells us that he takes pleasure in three things that are beautiful in the sight of God and of mortals: agreement among brothers and sisters, friendship among neighbors, and a wife and a husband who live in harmony. Likewise, there are three kinds of people he hates and whose manner of life he loathes: a pauper who boasts, a rich person who lies, and an old fool who commits adultery (*Si* 25:1-2).

So three is a kind of fullness. Something that has a beginning, a middle and an end seems to have all its required parts.

Four

But the other number that came to represent completion was the one immediately after it, four. In an article entitled 'Trinity and Quaternity', Victor White OP wrote about Carl Jung's fascination with the number four. From the ancient world as from the artefacts of many cultures, four seems to represent fullness more often even than three: there are four seasons, four elements, four cardinal points of the compass; for Christians the cross has four quarters facing four ways and thus embracing the whole universe; there are four rivers in Paradise, the name of God is the tetragrammaton (the four-lettered name), there are four gospels, there are four cardinal virtues, and so on. The cosmos seems to be a four-quartered thing just as the mature human being is the foursquare man. Four represented solidity, reliability, firmness and completion.

Chapter 30 of the Book of Proverbs contains many examples of four fold popular wisdom. Let me recall just the best known one:

> three things are wonderful for me, four I do not understand: the way of an eagle in the sky, the way of a snake on a rock, the way of a ship on the high seas, and the way of a man with a girl (*Pr* 30:18-19).

Seven

Not surprisingly, perhaps, other numbers that attract are the numbers you get when you add or multiply three and four. Multiply them and you get twelve – twelve tribes of Israel, twelve apostles, twelve foundation stones in the foursquare city that is the heavenly Jerusalem. Add them and you get seven, and so the Christian tradition settled on seven sacraments, Thomas Aquinas presents a full account of the moral life in terms of the seven virtues of faith, hope, charity, prudence, justice, fortitude and temperance. And of course the tradition also decided that there are seven deadly or capital sins.

Seven or Eight?

Well, eventually the tradition decided there were seven. The earliest considerations of them speak of eight. The most important early sources are, in the East, Evagrius Pontus (345-399) and John Cassian (c.360-c.434) and, in the West, Gregory the Great (c.540-604), and each of them speaks of eight. An important text behind this is Luke 11:26 in which Jesus speaks of a demon returning to a house that has been swept and put in order, and bringing with him seven other spirits more evil than himself. When it eventually settled on seven, the Christian tradition must have done so, at least to some extent, under the influence of the fact that seven is one of those 'completion numbers' that human beings find comforting. Most people will have been taught that there are seven, namely pride, covetousness, lust, anger, gluttony, envy and sloth. Popular culture recognises these also with a number of films in recent years dealing with these vices.

So how did the original eight become seven? Evagrius lists vainglory as a vice distinct from pride. John Cassian follows him in this. Gregory the Great calls pride 'the queen of sins' and 'the root of all evil' from which spring the other seven vices. He also lists vainglory as one of the seven. Thomas Aquinas continues to think in terms of eight, pride being regarded as a kind of super-deadly sin and vainglory still there on the list of seven. More popularly, the attraction of seven won out and we find pride and vainglory eventually rolled into one. So Chaucer, Dante, John of the Cross, and many others write about what were to become well-known as 'the seven deadly sins'.

Sins which lead to others

They are called deadly because these are the ones that either provide us with grave matter or dispose us towards it. They can therefore easily draw us into mortal sin, killing the life of grace in the soul. They are called capital sins by analogy with cardinal virtues. As the great virtues entail other virtues so these sins entail other sins. These are the 'heads', other vices are the 'tails' that follow them. In fighting serpents the thing to do is to lop off the head. If you manage to do that you save yourself from a lot of

7

other dangers that are attached to it and depend upon it. Gregory's reflections on them come in his commentary on Job 39:24-25 which refers to a horse smelling a distant battle, 'the thunder of the captains and the shouting'. Gregory interprets this as the sound of human beings contending with the deadly sins, which are like generals, he says, each of them bringing an army with it.

William Shakespeare speaks of how vices are connected in his play *Pericles* (Act I, scene 1):

> One sin, I know, another doth provoke;
> Murder's as near to lust as flame to smoke;
> Poison and treason are the hands of sin,
> Ay, and the targets to put off shame...

The attempt to develop a system of vices that would correspond to the structure of virtues is, however, doomed. To grow in virtue means to grow in coherence and consistency, to become integrated and directed in the spiritual life. Vice, *vitium* in Latin, refers to any sort of defect. Although we tend to think of vices as bad dispositions opposed to virtues which are good dispositions, vice has the character more of dissolution than of disposition, of things falling apart rather than things coming together even if it is only for the purpose of wickedness that they do come together. Although the idea of a capital sin is that it entails other sins (*Summa theologiae* I.II 73 1), Aquinas speaks for the entire Christian tradition in saying that there is no 'supreme evil' rivalling the 'supreme good' (*Summa theologiae* I 49 3). There is no 'final evil' to draw all things together. There is no organic 'kingdom of evil' as there is a kingdom of good, the body of Christ that renews all creation (*Summa theologiae* III 8 7-8).

In other words vice is about fragmentation, disorder, confusion and incoherence. Vices do not exist in their own names, as if they were realities added to the soul or to its faculties as the virtues are. Vices refer to the soul inhibiting itself, perhaps habitually, limiting itself from the perfection to which it should be moving. So vices are classified in terms of their opposition to virtues and not in their own right. This makes sense for a tradition for which evil is understood as a privation, a lack or absence of a good that ought to be there. Culpability attaches not to 'the vice' as if it were itself a moral agent, culpability attaches to the act from which it originates and to which it gives rise. That means it belongs to us as the moral agents whose acts are either virtuous or vicious.

Gregory the Great says there is a kind of reasonableness with which these vices exhort the conquered heart – don't be too hard on yourself, take up the cross but within reason, and so on. They can even tinge themselves with the colour of virtues, he says, and are more abominable the less they are known to be vices.

The struggle

There is a lot of wisdom, philosophical and theological, psychological and spiritual, gathered round the accounts of the deadly sins that have been offered by theologians and spiritual teachers. The tradition has lots to offer about these sins, from the fathers of the desert who often describe their assaults in the most florid terms, to John of the Cross who begins his *Dark Night of the Soul* by reminding those who would give themselves to prayer that they will need to find their way through subtle and persistent difficulties connected with these sins.

The fact that John of the Cross, at the point in his work when he is about to speak about the highest levels of spiritual experience, should turn again to talk about the seven deadly sins is an important reminder of their power and of the fact that we can never presume to be beyond their reach. Most of us know that we are not beyond the reach of at least some of them but the faults and weaknesses we know about are no trouble compared with the ones that remain hidden, camouflaged by our virtues and by the vices we accept in ourselves. In fact, to return to Luke 11:26, it is in a house that has been swept and put in order that the deadly sins happily make themselves at home. This is also, as we will see, why pride is so insidious.

They must be quite active in our communities, these deadly sins. If they are not it is because they are already triumphant and are not troubled by anybody trying to be holy, trying to love as Jesus loved. John of the Cross says that anybody who does try to love as Jesus loved will be brought very quickly face to face with the imperfections in himself that are the result of these sins.

So let us think about each in turn, to see how we might understand the origin and characteristics of each one in us.

Covetousness

The root of all evil

Traditionally pride is mentioned first. It is, as Gregory the Great puts it, the queen of the vices. Thomas Aquinas follows him in regarding pride as the sin of sins and Sirach 10:13 supported him in this. On the other hand, Dorothy Sayers entitles her account 'the other six deadly sins' on the grounds that everybody knows lust is a deadly sin but not everybody may know what the other six are. Here, though, we begin with covetousness, also called 'avarice' and 'greed', taking our cue from some texts in the Scriptures that see it as the root of all sin, especially from 1 Timothy 6:10 which says that 'the love of money is the root of all evil'.

Why is it the root of all evil, when it is concerned with just one aspect or area of life – wealth, property, belongings, what we can own? Avarice, surely, is simply undue attachment to things. Cassian thinks it ought to cause little trouble to any sincere and dedicated monk – just give away everything you have, do not keep anything for yourself, and away you go. The words of Jesus to the rich young man are taken as a charter for this aspect of monastic life: sell all you have, give the money to the poor, and follow Jesus. Simple. Or is it? It might be okay for monks but what about ordinary people who have to manage in the 'real world', worry about their family's health and prosperity, store up something for the rainy days yet to come?

As he normally does, Thomas Aquinas uses ideas from the writings of Aristotle to give a fairly humane, philosophical account of avarice. It means, he says, seeking to possess material wealth beyond the degree necessary to a life suited to one's station. It is a matter of proportion then, of having possessions within reason and using material things reasonably, in line with what one really needs. Questions of justice and charity come into it. Aquinas says, for example, that it is impossible for one person to enjoy extreme wealth without someone else suffering extreme want. And if people begin to find their sense of meaning and identity in external goods then reality is being distorted and we are faced with a potentially serious vice.

The scriptures are clear that covetousness is a radical thing. The text of 1 Timothy 6:10 has already been cited. Ephesians 5:5 and Colossians 3:5 regard greed as equivalent to idolatry, worship of a false god. Other biblical texts associate greed with injustice and with sexual immorality (for example, Sirach 14:9; Ezekiel 22:23-31; Amos 5:10-15; 1 Corinthians 10:6). Aquinas, who seems quite realistic about it as we have seen, notes that it is a capital sin not because it is obviously very bad in itself but because it provides the means for so many other sins to be carried out.

This is beginning to seem more serious, more fundamental. In the gospel we find Jesus saying 'blessed are you who are poor' and 'woe to you who are rich' (*Lk* 6:20,24). He says 'it is easier for a camel to pass through the eye of a needle than for a rich man to enter the kingdom of heaven' (*Lk* 18:25). He does not talk about 'undue attachment to wealth' or 'disproportionate interest in wealth': riches themselves are a problem, a point emphasised particularly in Luke's gospel.

You cannot serve both God and mammon. If what one owns becomes the source of one's meaning and identity, provides one's sense of self and one's sense of purpose, becomes the final goal of one's life, then something has gone seriously wrong. If the possession of things is no longer just about security and comfort but becomes a matter of identity and meaning then it is very likely to get in the way of our relating to God as we ought. God is to be our only treasure and our entire security. This is not a recommendation that we become impractical about the necessities of life, just that we live our lives within this radical, theological perspective.

We need to be alert to the ways in which the deadly sins can disguise themselves. They are skilled, the early teachers say, in presenting themselves as reasonable, even as virtuous, insinuating themselves into our lives under a

14

cover of good sense and moderation. They may play themselves off against each other. Concern about lust, for example, can lead us to neglect more serious matters, covetousness among them. Shakespeare's Macduff says that 'avarice strikes deeper, grows with more pernicious root / Than summer-seeming lust, and it hath been / the sword of our slain kings' (*Macbeth*, Act IV, scene 3).

God does not expect the impossible from us. We must be sensible, reasonable, and prudent. On the other hand how are we to continue to hear and respond to the gospel's radical call and acknowledge the extent to which covetousness can lead us away from the right path? Different kinds of relationship with material things are appropriate for people with different responsibilities and duties. At the same time every Christian is called to follow Christ in his poverty and to count no other treasure before him.

Money is not the only currency that gives people security, standing, meaning and identity. Anything we can claim to 'have' or to 'own' can function as a way of being rich. Knowledge, for example, is such a thing, and so is power or fame or high position. Gregory the Great speaks of this and Aquinas quotes him on it. Shakespeare speaks of workmen who strive to do better than well and end up 'confound(ing) their skill in covetousness' (*King John*, Act IV, scene 2). The ambition to own can even reach the point of enslaving people.

15

Spiritual Covetousness

What we might call spiritual wealth, the riches of theological, spiritual and cultural traditions, can be used in a way that is covetous. Anything can begin to function as property and to the extent that it does so our attachment to it can become idolatrous: we are finding our security and identity in something less than God. John of the Cross speaks about the ways in which spiritual wealth can be desired and used avariciously (*Dark Night* I, chapter 3). What he calls 'spiritual avarice' is seen where people become discontented with the spirituality God has given them. They want nothing except to listen to talks and to read books about spirituality instead of doing penance and perfecting inward poverty. Other people burden themselves with pictures, statues and rosaries, turning things that should help them to pray into a kind of possession to be held onto jealously. People can become collectors of religious objects, even of religious experiences, and there can be a subtle form of avarice in this.

John condemns 'the attachment of the heart, and the affection which they have for the nature, multitude and curiosity of these things'. It is, he says, 'quite contrary to poverty of spirit, which considers only the substance of devotion, makes use only of what suffices for that end and grows weary of this other kind of multiplicity and curiosity'. As long as we are imperfect we will have affections and attachments that are inappropriate. Only God's grace can heal us completely of such affections and attachments although we must do all we can to try to facilitate that process.

Avarice, greed, covetousness will want us to find our security and identity in possessions. It is a way of becoming self-sufficient and is thus a root of sin (*Ac* 14:15-17; *Rm* 1:19). Anger may arise from tiredness, lust from uncontrolled passion. But covetousness is cold and hostile, giving birth to lying, fraud, robbery, perjury and violence (Cassian), to treachery, deceit, restlessness and hardness of heart (Gregory). It goes too far in keeping things and too far in getting things, Aquinas says, and it is the most deforming of sins because it makes human desires subject to external things. Gregory the Great sees the tragedy of it: 'When the disturbed heart has lost the satisfaction of joy within it seeks for sources of consolation without, and is more anxious to possess external goods, the more it has no joy on which to fall back within.'

The amount of shopping that goes on, particularly on what used to be the Lord's Day, is thus an indication of how unhappy people are.

Envy

John Cassian does not mention envy explicitly when he lists the capital sins. Its place is taken by what he calls *tristitia*, sadness. In fact he discusses two kinds of sadness, the *tristitia* just mentioned and *acedia*, which is closer to listlessness or sloth. This is the sadness of disappointment and the first is a sadness that leads to bitterness. This bitter sadness is envy, 'lean-faced in her loathsome cave' as Shakespeare puts it. It is a difficult, insidious, persistent and destructive feeling and attitude.

Gregory the Great does call envy by its name, *invidia*. For him envy shows itself in resentment and anger that other people have good things I do not have. Where covetousness focuses on the things we might have which would give us a sense of identity, security and meaning, envy is our resentment at the other people who have those things. It shows itself in those feelings of emptiness and humiliation that other peoples' success and good fortune can arouse in us.

Envy and ambition

Envy is reasonable at first, presenting itself as legitimate ambition, but quickly transforms itself into something quite different. Why should I not aspire to what the other

18

person has, especially when it is something genuinely good? In any case why should there be inequalities among us? And if I cannot succeed in having what the other person has, and doing what they do, then why should they have and do those things either?

Beginning then in comparing ourselves with others, envy will try to rationalise and justify itself as a form of justice: it is about eliminating inequality and placing everybody on the same footing. When that does not work, however, it turns nasty. Instead of trying to lift myself to the level I admire in others, I decide instead to pull them down to my level. If I cannot also have that praise and success, then nobody else is going to have it either. So I gossip about people and question their motives or their real worth. I am happy to hear things that bring them down and am annoyed when I hear them well spoken of. I rejoice in their misfortune and am afflicted by their prosperity.

And who can deny that these are things found wherever human beings live and work together? For Saint James the root of problems in human communities is 'bitter envy and selfish ambition' (*Jm* 3:14,16). Shakespeare once again expresses things with admirable brevity and power: 'where envy breeds unkind division / There comes the rain, there begins confusion' (*Henry VI Part I*, Act IV, scene 1).

A type of sadness

Thomas Aquinas and John of the Cross follow the earlier teachers and understand envy as a sadness we experience at the good things others have and enjoy, especially their reputation and the regard in which they are held. Why is it that I should feel diminished by the talents and success of others? This is envy and it is clean contrary to charity because when I do love another person, and count them as my friend, I take pride in their talents and success. Those talents and success I regard as my own when it is my friend that is in question. As Saint Paul reminds us, love is not envious, and does not rejoice in the wrong. But when I begin to envy my friend his gifts and success it is clear that I have 'fallen out of friendship' with him. I am no longer his friend. I no longer love him. There is now a distance between us. Rather than something in which I too might take pride, his good fortune has become a threat to me. It is only a short step then to hating him. Hate, of course, is another way of being passionate about somebody, of having him under my skin. The hatred that sprouts from envy is very destructive. It is already destructive of the one who envies and it presents huge problems for living together: 'there comes the rain, there begins confusion'.

In a different way, envy is opposed to mercy. Mercy arises from yet another kind of sadness, the sadness I feel at another person's misfortune. Envy is the sadness I feel at another person's good fortune. Thomas Aquinas believes we are more likely to envy those close to us rather than those who are distant. We envy those with whom we can compare ourselves as colleagues and contemporaries, brothers and sisters, those whose successes and achievements we regard as potentially within our own reach. It is not impossible that there would be envy between people of quite varying roles and situations in life though Aquinas thinks it is more likely between people who regard themselves as equals in some sense.

The feelings of humiliation, diminishment and exclusion that accompany envy are very difficult to handle and will sometimes seem overwhelming. Inability to understand and manage such feelings is a major factor in the death of friendship and is a major factor also leading to violence in human affairs. The second chapter of the Book of Wisdom gives a clear account of how this process works: the good person, simply by being good, provokes envy and hatred in others who (irrationally) take his or her goodness as a reproach to themselves. It is an important background text for understanding the experience of Jesus and his rejection, the just one whose presence is intolerable in a sinful, envious world.

In modern times the psychoanalyst Melanie Klein placed envy at the centre of her account of human development. Her work with children and troubled adults led her to regard envy as the fundamental reality in human relationships. She believed it to be something innate, almost like an original sin in human nature. Envy gets in the way of gratitude. The bitter sadness of envy prevents us appreciating the reality of grace. If the truth be told, we do not really want grace. We do not really want to be indebted, to be needy, to be cared for. We resent the ones who are good to us. This is what Klein saw clearly in the responses of very young children. Shakespeare puts the same insight on the lips of Cardinal Wolsey: 'you turn the good we offer into envy' (*Henry VIII*, Act III, Scene 1). We envy the good person their goodness even as they share it with us, not just when they are sharing it with others. This is the strange sadness and stubborn ingratitude of envy.

Grudging a brother his grace

Aquinas saw this also. One of the fruits of envy was described as 'grudging a brother his grace'. Aquinas believes this is in fact the sin against the Holy Spirit, in which a person envies the Holy Spirit. Imagine envying the Holy Spirit! Using her own terms, Melanie Klein spoke about envy of 'the good breast', which is, I suppose, a metaphor we might use in talking about God's Holy Spirit. In the case of envy it seems straightforward enough to bring together the contemporary psychological insight and the traditional theological one.

Envy is likely to be a major difficulty, then, wherever people strive to grow in charity, to love one another. Dorothy Sayers says that envy will be content where all are equally unhappy. I'm afraid I did live once in a community, a religious community, where that seemed to be the preferred option of some of its members: shared unhappiness was preferable to any real joy!

It is clearly urgent that Christians who would be witnesses to grace should think long and hard about what grace means, and how human beings might dispose themselves towards it. We need to think long and hard too about envy as a key enemy of grace – as the Parson says in *The Canterbury Tales*, 'envy is the worst sin: all other sins are only against one virtue whereas envy is against all virtue and against all goodness'.

Sloth

A Dominican colleague told me that he had spent fifteen years working on a doctoral dissertation on the deadly sin of sloth. He believed that by the end he was the world's leading authority on sloth, both theoretically and practically. We can presume that the reason it took him so long was because he was drawn into pastoral and teaching responsibilities that prevented him working fulltime on his doctorate: at least we can hope so!

A disappointed sadness

Sloth is the English term used for *acedia*, the other kind of sadness to which John Cassian refers, a sadness that is disappointed rather than bitter and perhaps even sometimes despairing. *Acedia* is referred to also as the noonday devil, the kind of listlessness that comes with the heat of high noon. Envy is bitter whereas sloth is disappointed and disillusioned. The term is found in the Latin translations of Sirach 6:25: 'do not fret (*non acedieris*) under the bonds of wisdom', it tells us (see also *Ps* 37:1, 7, 8 and *Pr* 24:19). This kind of fretting, a mixture of anxiety and melancholy, arises not in view of my neighbour's blessings – that kind of resentful sadness is envy, as we have seen – but in view of the demands the divine blessing makes on me.

John Cassian says it is a vice well known to monks and hermits. Even when they are far away from people and events, sloth is present because it arises from inside, in the struggles of the 'inner man.' Gregory the Great calls it melancholy, *melancholia*. When the mind loses the sweetness of tranquillity, he says, nothing supports it but the grief resulting from agitation. Hence the strange kind of fruitless disquiet that comes with it, the restlessness and distraction. We re-order our books and change the furniture round. And when we have finished, we do it again. We flick aimlessly through the television channels.

A call to grow up

For John of the Cross, losing the consolations of God throws people into this kind of sadness. People give up prayer then, he says, find nothing in it and get nothing out of it. They would have God will what they will, he continues, and are fretful of having to will that which God wills, finding it repugnant to accommodate their will to that of God. Their aim is spiritual sweetness and consolation ('to remain at the breast' is his way of putting it). They are too weak to have the fortitude for, and to bear the trials of, perfection. Softly nurtured, they run fretfully from everything that is hard and take offence at the cross. But it is not possible to enter on the narrow way without sorrow and repugnance. What is happening, John continues, is a kind of spiritual weaning, God removing the breasts of sweetness and pleasure to free us from irrelevancies and puerilities, giving us bitter herbs to prepare us for the spiritual food of adult believers.

The noonday devil

For Thomas Aquinas sloth is called the noonday devil because it strikes at noon, at the mid-point. 'Noon' refers, he says, not simply to the time of day but to the mid-point of any project, journey or undertaking. We groan about not being more fruitful and 'think that other, distant monasteries are better off than we are'. This can be applied across the board: other families, other marriages, other schools, other neighbourhoods, other generations have it easier, are more interesting and rewarding, than the time at which we must live, the place in which we must live and the people with whom we must live. It prevents us being content with what is 'here and now' because 'there and then' always seems better. An oppressive sorrow, it depresses the spirit so that we do not want to do anything. It sorrows particularly over spiritual goods, Aquinas says, even the divine good. At its worst sloth means being disgusted with spiritual and divine things.

The fruits of sloth

Although it is often understood simply as laziness, the fruits of sloth are capable of great damage. Those fruits have been identified as malice, spite, pusillanimity (or cowardice), despair, sluggishness, idleness and distraction, agitation of mind, restlessness of body, instability, verbosity and curiosity. It is clear that sloth is a kind of psychological or spiritual 'black hole': there is energy but it is falling away into a sterile, unproductive place. In sloth the mind collapses in on itself and self-hatred is not far away.

Dorothy Sayers identifies the disguises of sloth as tolerance to the point of indifference and 'a whiffling activity of the body'. The latter is much ado about nothing, workaholism, violent or dramatic activity in the hope of escaping from the horrors of sloth, its spiritual emptiness.

How to manage sloth

How is it to be managed? The best way to manage sloth is through charity. Love, once again and not surprisingly, is the solution. Sloth, like the other deadly and capital sins is a sin against charity. This one is specifically against the joy of charity and so it is driven out by charity itself. Concretely, it is managed in two ways according to Thomas Aquinas. One is through steady thought, *cogitatio perseverans*. Alban McCoy says sloth 'puts a brake on thinking'; Aquinas says that the way to get out of it is by releasing that brake and thinking well about things. The other way to manage sloth is through taking 'sabbath', proper rest. Sloth is a sin against the third commandment because it does not allow us to rest our minds in God.

One startling idea in what Aquinas says is that sloth 'amputates the voice'. It paralyses people and strikes them dumb, freezing the external members of the body and especially the voice, which most expresses interior thoughts and feelings. It seems clear then that helping or allowing or encouraging a person to find their voice, to give voice to their thoughts and feelings, must also be a way of managing this sadness. This is part of the Christian ministry of mutual encouragement: seeking ways to put courage into one another so that we will continue the journey and not be dismayed by the difficulties we may face.

To speak of mutual encouragement is to speak once again of charity, in its acts of spiritual accompaniment and fraternal correction, of counselling and friendship, providing the kinds of spaces in which people can be encouraged to think and speak and be heard. Many of the symptoms of *acedia* will be recognised as those that accompany depression: the listlessness, pointlessness, and meaninglessness; the resistance very often to the suggestions of friends trying to stimulate them into thought or action, to lift them out of it by proposing good things to them. When a person is depressed it can be very difficult if not impossible to 'lift their spirits'. Conversation with a friend, Aquinas says, is one of the main ways to get beyond this kind of paralysing sadness.

Finding hope

The task is to give people hope, to get them to see that there is a way out of the trap in which they find themselves. The best way to do this, John of the Cross implies, is to get people to give up measuring God by themselves and instead to measure themselves by God. This is what it means to enter into the theological virtue of hope, to live in God's infinite 'space' and eternal 'time', the best possible 'here and now' which is already ours if we are prepared to embrace the cross so as to enjoy its fruits. Saint Paul warns that people may be overwhelmed by excessive sorrow (2 Co 2:7) but reminds his readers that there is a godly grief that produces repentance leading to salvation as well as a worldly grief that produces death (2 Co 7:10). The latter, we may conclude, is Paul's recognition that the feelings and attitudes associated with sloth, which are always psychologically deadening, may sometimes be spiritually fatal as well. The other, godly grief is what later spiritual teachers value as 'the gift of tears', a melting of the hard places of the heart, tears that bring fresh energy and new joy.

Gluttony

Can you meditate if you are not a vegetarian? This was a question put to me by a beautiful young lady on a school retreat in Trinidad many years ago. I was preparing to speak to her class about meditation and different ways of praying. She interrupted me before I began, told me that her grandfather was a Hindu teacher, and said that he had told her that one could not meditate properly without being a vegetarian.

Her question has stayed with me ever since. The tradition of vegetarianism is very strong in all ascetical and monastic regimes, including Christian ones. Some of the first teachers of Christian monasticism, Evagrius and John Cassian for example, name gluttony as the first of the deadly sins. In Cassian's case it is first because it is the root or spring of all the others. For Evagrius, spiritual contemplation, the goal of the monk, is attained only where there is freedom not only from passions of the soul but from passions of the body also.

The most carnal sin

To rank gluttony as a deadly sin may seem unreasonable. It is a carnal, warm-hearted, or natural sin, according to

30

Cassian and Gregory (as are lust and anger also). Gregory seems quite understanding in relation to it: it comes last in his list because it is, he says, the least radical of the deadly sins. Cassian agrees that it is a carnal or warm-hearted sin, not as vicious or as consciously wicked as the cold-hearted deadly sins, but at the same time it is first in his list. He ranks them from the most carnal to the most spiritual but believes that each grows out of the one that precedes it. This means gluttony is not only the first, it is the root of all the deadly sins, the spring from which they all ultimately flow. The original sin of Adam and Eve is partly a sin of gluttony, Cassian says, and the first temptation the devil places before Jesus is a temptation to gluttony. So the Christian has to guard especially against it. Hence the importance of fasting and other bodily discipline if one is to remain faithful to prayer and the spiritual life.

Because it is a carnal, fleshly sin, thought alone will not be enough to manage gluttony. A pattern or way of living is needed, a regime by which to live one's life. This regime must include fasting, keeping vigil, works of penance and living in a remote place. (Cassian is thinking of monks in the first place: we have to apply it to other Christian vocations as appropriate. The Dominicans, for example, once followed an austere regime of fasting, abstinence from meat and other penances. But their vocation to preach the gospel was not compatible with 'living in a remote place'.) When we recall that, for

Cassian, gluttony is the root of the other vices it is easy to understand why he emphasises fasting: it is crucial to the struggle with all the vices.

Types of gluttony

Cassian speaks of three kinds of gluttony: eating out of hours, eating anything and everything, and being fussy about what one eats. Later teachers identified five kinds, where people ate hastily, sumptuously, daintily, excessively or greedily. It is important not to embarrass one's host, and this is one of the reasons why gluttonous eating is offensive. One's own taste is not necessarily that of others and it would be offensive to try to impose it on others. Gluttony is not just a matter of quantity (whether one is eating more than one reasonably needs), or of etiquette at the table (whether one is eating hastily or greedily). It is also about remembering others: thinking about one's host, thinking about one's table partners, thinking about the poor.

According to Sigmund Freud, there is an 'oral' stage of human development which if not successfully negotiated leaves people with difficulties later on. These difficulties can express themselves in addictive behaviour, not only but especially in relation to food and drink. Anorexia, bulimia and alcoholism are all serious psychological and physical problems and are in a different class to simple, vicious gluttony. But in relation to such problems it is important to remember Cassian's insight that thought alone is not a solution to difficulties in this area. A pattern or way of living needs to be set in place that will ensure good health physically, psychologically and morally.

Temperance

Alcohol poses special problems. For Thomas Aquinas problematic liquors are those that produce 'fumes to confuse the head'. A special virtue is needed to manage the particular challenges posed by such liquors, the virtue he calls sobriety. He is not a puritan about it, not even a teetotaller: such liquors should be used moderately and with care about the consequences. There is even an opposed vice, rare in matters of temperance, which he calls unfeelingness or insensitivity. It means an inability to enter into human celebration. On the opposite side to drunkenness and other forms of gluttony, this inability may be not only a psychological and social problem, it might even be a moral fault. 'If a person knows', Aquinas says, 'that his abstinence lays an oppressive burden on human nature, then he is not without sin'.

In a short catechism, *The Teaching of the Catholic Church*, Herbert McCabe summarises admirably Aquinas's very reasonable and wise understanding of what temperateness requires in matters of food and drink:

240. We exercise the virtue of temperateness in the matter of eating and drinking by, characteristically,

taking and enjoying what is sufficient for our health and for the entertainment of our friends.

241. We may fail (in the exercise of temperateness in this area) by indifference to the enjoyments of the table; by eating and drinking that is totally divorced from either friendship or the requirements of health; by eating what is merely superficially attractive at the expense of a reasonable diet, by drug abuse and by all forms of gluttony and drunkenness.

The heavenly banquet

Human beings, as living animals, must eat and drink enough to sustain their life and their health. Not only that, the Christian faith encourages us to look forward to a great banquet, a feast of fine wines and the best food, a never-ending (it seems) wedding banquet. Christ himself becomes our food. Union with him and with his Father in the Spirit is, in the words of John of the Cross, 'the supper that refreshes love'. Christ is the bread of life, God's wisdom, who invites us to feast on him, to savour his teaching, to digest it and make it our own. He is the living bread whose flesh and blood are given for the life of the world, the bread of the Eucharist his flesh to be eaten (chewed, as Saint John's gospel startlingly tells us), the wine of the Eucharist his blood poured out for all and to be drunk by all who wish to have a part in him.

So eating and drinking are part not just of the natural order of our lives, they are part of the supernatural order of our lives. Gluttonous ways of eating and drinking would see us, like animals gathering at feeding time. But human beings eat rather than feed: a meal is always, or ideally ought to be, a social, friendship-building moment. The greatest betrayal is not that of an enemy but that of a friend, of one who 'ate his bread with me'.

Consumerism

But we need to be careful not to become indulgent towards ourselves in relation to food and drink. The culture in which most of us now live is often described as 'consumerist'. The problems of climate change and other environmental concerns have alerted us to the devouring, rapacious side of the human being. We exploit and consume the world's resources without proper thought. Yesterday's luxuries become today's necessities as the market creates new needs and desires in people. Dorothy Sayers wrote about this already in the 1940s, how advertising flatters and frightens us out of a reasonable contentment into greedy hankering for goods we do not really need. 'The cooperative gluttony of the consumer', she says, 'keeps up the whirligig of industrial finance based on gluttonous consumption'. It is important to enjoy the good things of life. It is just as important to be alert to ways in which this might blunt our sensitivity to matters of justice and charity.

Lust

Lust cannot refer simply to sexual desire. The living animal experiences sexual desire just as it experiences hunger and thirst. Human beings are living animals. Not only that, but the living human animal is the image and likeness of God.

The origins of lust

Plato devotes his dialogue *Symposium* to a discussion of love. One of the contributors famously proposes that the separation of the sexes and their yearning for each other is the outcome of a fall from an original plan. In the beginning it was not so but for some reason things changed and it is as we experience it now. *Eros* has become part of human experience, a yearning for 'the other' who will be the perfect match, our 'other half'.

Gregory of Nyssa took seriously the idea that sexual difference arose as a result of a fall from the state God originally intended for us. It might quickly come to mind that Genesis 1:26-28 already speaks about God creating the human being 'male and female', in God's own image and likeness, and this is before there is any question of a fall. Ah, says Gregory, this was because God anticipated what was to happen. God created them as male and female, giving them organs for sexual reproduction, because God knew they would fall from grace and so end up needing the sexual organs with which he had equipped them from the beginning!

Thomas Aquinas disagreed firmly and clearly with Gregory on this and said that our sexual desire and capacity are part of the original and good creation, that before the fall Adam and Eve might have enjoyed sex (and enjoyed it far more, Thomas says, than anybody can now do) and conceived children, just as they presumably ate of the good things of the garden before they ate the fruit that was forbidden. He also says that one of the ways in which the human being is in the image of God is in our capacity to reproduce: as God is from God, in the generation of the Word and procession of the Spirit, so human beings come from human beings. It means there is a fuller 'imaging' of God in the living human animal than there is in the angel which is purely (and therefore only) spiritual.

Sexuality in context

Alban McCoy writes well about lust, taking account of much contemporary understanding of human sexuality as well as the contemporary Catholic theology of marriage. He puts it well: we are to live lustily but not lustfully. So when does sexual desire become lustful, when does it become sinful? It depends on the context in which it is acted upon – by whom, with whom, in what way. The desire itself cannot automatically be sinful. Acting on it may be sinful depending on how it is done and with whom. It depends on the commitments and relationships people have made. Sexual activity should be appropriate to who we are and what we are about. It has to be respectful of human dignity in ourselves and in others.

The tradition links lust and gluttony. The physical organs involved are situated close to each other, some of the early teachers point out, and gluttony gives rise to lust. We can also think about it in this way: to treat a person lustfully is a way of chopping them up into manageable bits with a view to incorporating them into ourselves. Lust loses sight of the other person as a human person, makes them something less than that, and is happy then to 'have' them with a view to its own pleasure. It acts without proper thought for the person in front of it as also without proper thought for the third person, the potential child, which the sexual drive is always also about.

So marriage is the place for sexual activity – this is Catholic teaching – and nowhere else. It is not absolutely impossible that a person may, by God's grace, live always in perfect chastity. That does not mean never having sex. It means living our sexuality in ways appropriate to our commitments and relationships: in truth and in love. But such perfect chastity seems practically impossible for most people, and for three reasons: the strength of this desire, the fragmentation of human nature, and the things human beings need to learn about intimacy, life and love.

Discipline and humour

So what are we to do? We are to live in a way that combines strong discipline with a sense of humour. John Cassian speaks well about the discipline. Like gluttony, this is a warm-hearted vice, he says, deeply rooted in our physical nature, and so not susceptible to management by thought alone. 'The mind's attentiveness is not enough of itself', he writes, 'bodily discipline must come to its assistance: fasting, vigils and works of penance', as well as meditation on Scripture and constant watchfulness.

There are two difficulties with Cassian. One of the strategies he recommends for coping with lust (as with gluttony) is to live in a remote place. This is okay for monks and hermits. The vocation of most people, though, places them in the midst of the Church and of the world, among people, some of whom they are bound to find very attractive, some of whom they will probably fall in love with from time to time, and some of whom may even find them attractive (surprising as that often is).

The other difficulty – though Cassian is far from being the worst in this – is a kind of deadly seriousness about sexual matters that can have the opposite to its desired effect, a puritanism and fear of the body which needs to be avoided in case people go completely mad. Cassian does suggest that vainglory is a cure for lust and this may be his idea of a joke. What he means is that people may be tempted to take pride in their ability to control their sexual desires: here's a motivation that will help people to manage lust, something to be proud of, something that makes one different from other people...the danger is clear. Because vainglory is also a capital vice, keeping lust in its place for reasons of vainglory may be a matter of 'out of the frying pan into the fire' – or perhaps into some kind of fridge, since vainglory and pride are cold-hearted sins.

Dorothy Sayers says that people fall into lust for two reasons. One is because of the sheer exuberance of animal spirits. In regard to this, a sharp application of the curb may be all that is needed to bring the body into subjection and remind it of its proper place in the scheme of human nature, spiritual as well as bodily. Calm discipline, then, and a sense of humour. The other reason people fall into lust, she thinks, is through sheer boredom and discontent. People give in to lust 'because they have nothing better to do'. The context of people's lives is crucial here.

Life, love and intimacy

Sexual desire is about life and love and intimacy. A human life without these things is unbearable. Lust – sexual desire out of context and therefore destined to lead us astray – is best managed indirectly, through putting in place other things that fill our lives with intimacy, life and love. What is meant are things like friendship, fulfilling work, relaxation, enjoyment of nature, music, art and prayer. Because we are sensual beings we must live sensual lives. Where people's mental and physical surroundings are drab and uncomfortable, where the philosophy they are offered is bankrupt (in particular the myths about sex that the modern world pedals), where people's vitality is impoverished and their culture superficial, then they will fall into a spiritual depression, Sayers says, from which the satisfaction of lust provides some partial, temporary release.

Sometimes, in giving way to lust, people are genuinely seeking love but the two of course are not to be confused. Shakespeare has many severe things to say about lust – it is 'a bloody fire', 'a cistern', 'wanton', 'monstrous' and 'shameful' – and contrasts beautifully the effects of love and lust:

> Love comforteth like sunshine after rain
> But lust's effect is tempest after sun
> Love's gentle spring doth always fresh remain
> Lust's winter comes ere summer half be done
> Love surfeits not, lust like a glutton dies
> Love is all truth, lust full of forged lies

> *- Venus and Adonis,* stanza 132

For Christians there is another level of intimacy, life and love, a fuller context in which everything is to be understood and lived out. This is the intimacy, life and love given in Christ's relationship with us, the friendship with the Father in the Holy Spirit that Christ establishes for us. The great moment in which this love is celebrated is the Eucharist. It ought not to be surprising then, that, people have the interest they have in the liturgy which, although it is a public work of the Church, is the moment of greatest intimacy with Our Lord, where our love is sealed and our life increased, where all our desires are satisfied. The bread from heaven contains in itself all delights, the liturgy says. It is the place where we realise that 'the Other' with whom we seek to be united is the God in whose image we are created.

42

Anger

According to some passages in the Bible anger is a very good thing. According to others it can be a very bad thing. In James 1:20 we read that the righteousness of God is never served by the anger of men. In Matthew 5:22 Jesus teaches his disciples that everyone who is angry with his brother will be liable to judgement, whoever insults his brother will be answerable to the council and whoever calls his brother a fool will be liable to the hell of fire.

The uses of anger

Jesus himself, though, was not always 'meek and mild'. At the heart of his public ministry, whether it happened at the beginning or towards the end of that ministry, is the cleansing of the temple. From time to time Jesus expresses his frustration with the disciples. The curses against the Pharisees in Matthew 23 are colourful and uncompromising. Many passages throughout the Scriptures speak about the zeal, wrath and vengeance of the Lord, the God of Israel. There is then ambivalence and complexity in what is said about anger.

In his book *Enthusiasm*, Ronald Knox concludes that the dangers of enthusiasm in religion are clear and its disasters have been many but that if nobody ever got enthusiastic about anything, Christianity would be inert, effectively dead. So it is with anger. Its dangers are clear (violence, insults, uproar) and its disasters are many but without it where would we be? Well, according to Saint John Chrysostom, without anger sound doctrine would not be advanced or good judgement maintained or crime put down.

The concern of anger is justice and injustice and so, Aquinas says, it is the passion most closely linked with reason, with thought, inference and deduction. It is the passion that ought to accompany vindication, where injustices are undone and the balance of justice restored. Of course anger can easily be placed at the service of revenge rather than vindication. It can precede and supplant thought rather than serve it. Dorothy Sayers says that the energy of anger can be harnessed and driven by cold-headed and cold-hearted envy, avarice and pride. But an old saying has it that *abusus non tollit usum*, the abuse of something does not take away from its right use. The energy of good anger is at work every day, in every area of life, anger at the service of justice.

Categorising anger

Anger is a passion that has no contrary and this too makes it difficult to understand. Is it any wonder we would be apprehensive about it when its nature is uncertain? The reason it has no contrary, according to Aquinas, is that it contains contrariety within itself. In anger there is both pain and sadness. You know how amazed we can be at people who in their hurt hit out in anger to hurt others but do not realise the hurt they cause or, if they do, are incapable of believing it is comparable to their own. Anger is complex, including both desire and hope, the first a straightforward, desiring passion and the second a more complex, striving passion.

There are three kinds of anger according to the classical sources on the deadly sins. One is a surge of anger that is kept within and that passes quickly. A second is an anger that for the most part remains within but which is held onto, cherished, not easily left behind. And the third kind is the anger that breaks out in words or deeds.

The first blazes up interiorly, Cassian says, and is called *thumos* in Greek. Aristotle calls this 'quick-tempered' anger. Gregory the Great calls it silent anger because it is contained within, John Damascene calls it wrath and Nemesius calls it gall. It is a passing squall of anger that flashes through a person but which the person manages to contain.

The second kind of anger is not finished in a short space of time but is held over for days and even longer. This, says Cassian, is called *menis* in Greek, and Aristotle refers to it as 'bitter-tempered' anger. John Damascene calls this kind mania or ill-will, Nemesius calls it mania meaning madness and Aquinas speaks of it as an anger that makes a person taciturn, silent, and immobile. He implies that if repressed it might even cause a person to die. This is where a person decides to hold on to their anger and to live from it, as it were, at least in relation to the person with whom they are angry. Held within, it is clearly psychologically unhealthy. Anger turned against the self leads to bitterness, melancholy and even worse. Suicide might on occasion be the ultimate outcome of this kind of anger.

The third kind is the anger that breaks out in word and deed. Cassian says this kind is called *orge*. Gregory the Great calls it vocal or outspoken anger, Nemesius calls it rage and John Damascene rancour (*furor* in Latin). For this kind of extrovert, at times flamboyant anger Cicero uses the beautiful word *excandescentia*. In English we speak of people being incandescent with rage. Cicero suggests the term excandescent. This is Aristotle's 'harsh-tempered' anger.

Displaced anger

Anger is full of energy and it causes things to happen, some of them good and some of them not good. It is the most vehement and most forceful of the passions. Gregory the Great describes the effect of anger in the human being in a way that can be presented in the form of a hectic poem:

Heart beats quickly,
body trembles,
tongue stammers,
countenance is fired.
Eyes blaze
but familiar acquaintances are not recognised.
Lips sound
but one does not realise what one is saying.

While unjustified, disproportionate and unreasonable anger is a vice, it can also be morally wrong to lack anger where one ought to be righteously indignant. To be angry in accord with right reason is praiseworthy, Aquinas says. Never to get angry may mean that one does not care enough about things, about people, about events. There is a story about a man arriving in heaven with no wounds and being asked 'was nothing worth fighting for? nothing worth suffering for? nothing worth getting hurt for?' John of the Cross says that some souls are so patient as regards their progress that God would gladly see them less so.

Modern psychology adds much to our understanding of anger. One idea it develops is that of displacement: the man is angry with his wife who is angry with her child who is angry with the dog who is angry with the cat... One of the indications that a particular manifestation of anger might be sinful, Aquinas says, is when it is misdirected in this way. Although we are angry, we lack the courage (perhaps), to confront the real source and cause of our anger and take it out on someone weaker than that source and cause (sometimes this will be ourselves).

Projected anger

A second idea found in modern psychological accounts of anger (but already understood by John of the Cross, for example) is the idea of projection: we transfer onto others and place in them characteristics and qualities that we dislike in ourselves. John writes about people who are angry at the sins of others and who watch them with a sort of uneasy zeal (anger often manifests itself in religious people as 'uneasy zeal'). They set themselves up as masters of virtue, he says, and fail to see the mote in their own eye. They can be angry at the things about themselves that they dislike only if they place those things in others.

Anger is about the drive for vengeance and this may be rightly or wrongly directed just as it may be pursued in ways that may be morally praiseworthy or disproportionate and so sinful. It is a capital sin. When Aquinas speaks about it, for example, it is clear that he believes it is not automatically mortal, just that it inevitably brings other vices with it. It opens the door to many vices, perhaps even to all the vices (as a medieval gloss on *Pr* 29:22 says).

Turning anger to good

What is to be done about anger? To meditate on the gentleness of the angry Jesus and the anger of Jesus who was gentle opens us onto a more familiar theological question: how God who is infinitely merciful is, within that infinite mercy, also infinitely just. In the Scriptures there is much about God's mercy, love and compassion… there is more (it seems, at times) about God's jealous love, God's wrath and zeal, the great and terrible day when he will finally act against sin and injustice. Will he not see justice done for those who call upon Him and will he not see it done speedily? Yes, he will. There is power in anger. And so, already on the third day, the wrath of God was revealed in the resurrection of his Son from the dead.

Pride – and Vainglory

As mentioned in the first chapter, there is confusion in the tradition about whether there are eight or seven capital or deadly sins. Some of the Fathers speak of eight and use allegorical interpretations of Old Testament and New Testament texts in support. Deuteronomy 7:1, for example, speaks of the seven nations to be driven out of Canaan (who with the Egyptians make eight). Luke 11:26, as we have seen, tells of a wandering demon who decides to return to the house from which he had been driven out bringing seven others with him.

Where there are eight, pride is included along with vainglory. Where there are seven, these two are regarded as one. Thomas Aquinas, for example, follows Gregory the Great in taking vainglory as a capital vice opposed to magnanimity. Pride, on the other hand, is the queen of sins, opposed to humility and something that can attack any good thing. It is a kind of super-capital sin, more radical than the capital sins themselves. A mistranslation (as often happened) gave rise to a tradition of thinking about pride as queen of sins. Sirach 10:13 says that the beginning of pride is sin. Gregory's translation reversed it: the beginning of sin is pride.

Thinking about pride involves thinking about reality, about truth. Pride is out of touch with the truth and so is false and empty. Pride carries nothing more than 'the power of an empty name', Gregory says. The mind of a proud man, says the Book of Sirach, is 'like a decoy partridge in a cage' (11:30). What a strange image! A decoy partridge is all façade and no depth, not at all what it pretends to be, and such is pride the most spiritual of sins. Pride hinders our access to truth whereas humility makes for truth and wisdom.

Humility

Humility is from *humus*, meaning earth, and is lowly. It is not self-hatred but a willingness to allow the soil of our lives be ploughed over again, to allow our hearts and minds to be broken down anew. It means being docile, accepting that we still have everything to learn. Pride is from *hubris*, and refers to what is inflated. It is not so much a proper self-esteem and love as an over-reaching of oneself, being out of touch with the truth about oneself, being wanton in one's aspirations.

Paradoxically, our concern with how we are seen can lead us to avoid some sins. Vainglory can lead us to fast and to avoid fornication, because others see us, and we want to appear good or avoid shame. But concern with how we are seen can easily tip us into other sinful situations. Cassian thinks vainglory may save us from worse sins. Aquinas (thinking of it as pride rather than vainglory) says there is nothing worse than pride. In fact, he says, God allows people to fall into disgraceful sins in order to avoid their falling into pride. Evagrius had written that the person who is spiritually mature drives out evil thoughts not by calling up other evil thought incompatible with the first but by calling up thoughts of virtue.

Comparing with others

The story of the Pharisee and the publican in Luke 18:9-14 shows us how pride works. 'I am not like other men', says the Pharisee, and there's the rub. His point of comparison in evaluating his life and behaviour is other people. I am certainly better than others, he thinks. In fact God is the one with whom we ought to compare ourselves when evaluating our lives and behaviour. This is what the publican does, not daring even to lift his head towards the One with whom he compared himself. As I once heard a preacher put it, 'the humble person compares himself only with God and thereby knows his own nothingness and his own greatness'.

It was in a mistaken comparison of this sort that sin originated. 'You shall be like gods', the serpent promises Adam and Eve. Pride is the sin of thinking ourselves gods in a way that frees us from our indebtedness to God. It means trying to lay our hands on the greatness God intends to give us – to become partakers of the divine nature – and to take it as if it were ours by right.

Thomas Aquinas says that pride is an evaluation of oneself that is unreasonable, *praeter rationem*. That phrase, literally 'beside reason' or 'beyond reason', corresponds with the Greek phrase *para noia*. Pride is the most spiritual of sins. Its entire drama can be enacted inside our heads. This is closer to the normal meaning we give the English term 'paranoia', a drama enacted inside a person's head that has no basis in reality. Psychologists say that the human infant, at a certain point in its development, is omnipotent, all-powerful. Everybody and everything is obliged to dance to attention and to respond to its faintest squeal. He or she is adorable, we will even hear people say. It must be the case that this moment survives in us, at least in the memory of a power we might long to taste again, to be the centre of the universe.

But living with others, Cassian teaches, is a great help in all this. They will correct us if we get too distorted a view of ourselves. We are frequently rebuked by the presence of other people and although aggravations more readily appear where people live together they are also quickly remedied, he believed. God's providence will send things our way that will help us to remain humble.

Pride attacks our strength

Other sins are established on our weaknesses but it is our strengths that are attacked by pride and it is our strengths – gifts and talents in whatever area – that can easily lead to us becoming proud. When other vices and sins are rooted out, says Cassian, vainglory and pride spring up all the more vigorously. When we are victorious and triumphant, especially in spiritual matters, vainglory and pride come along.

Dorothy Sayers says we ought to distrust all high ambitions and lofty ideals, especially those that make the wellbeing of humanity their ultimate end. For then humanity is just the extension of my own ego and, if we do it in a spiritual or theological way, we may even find ourselves turning God into an instrument of human projects and intentions. 'The road to hell is paved with good intentions' can be understood, she says, to refer not to the intentions we have made which we have not carried out but to the intentions we have carried out, the ones we have pursued idealistically, the ones we have therefore deified and idolised, turning them into ends in themselves: my ideas, my choices, my plans.

Dominicans have some characteristic temptations to pride. (I can say this because it is the Order to which I belong and because I am pretty confident that other groups, nationalities, etc. take comparable pride in some aspects of their history or lifestyle.) 'We are not like other men', one hears Dominicans saying from time to time. (They will be thinking of rivals like the Jesuits perhaps!) 'Truth is our interest and our intention', you might well hear a Dominican say. What a dangerous intention, what a high aspiration. We need to keep watch lest it turn into a highway to hell. 'We are about study and learning', you might also hear the Dominican say. Yes, but immediately after his account of pride Aquinas speaks about the vice of curiosity, the disordered desire for knowledge. The proud learn from no one, he says. Humility is essential if we are to continue to grow in knowledge and wisdom whereas pride, delighting in its own excellence, grows bored with the excellence of truth.

Love is the answer

What will undo the pride of humans, Augustine asks. Cassian says that the experiences of life will help, especially the aggravations that accompany living with others. More radically though, says Augustine, it is the humility of God that undoes the pride of human beings. The one who, though he was in the form of God, did not count equality with God a thing to be grasped, but emptied himself taking the form of a servant, and became humble, even to death on a cross: it is he, Jesus, the Word made flesh, God-with-us, who teaches us what humility means. He shows that humility comes along with love.

The cure for all the deadly or capital sins, as for all sin, is love. Charity is the remedy in all cases, especially for the thornier issues with which human beings have to struggle, lust and pride for example. Saint Paul states clearly that love is the antidote to the deadly sins:

> Love is patient and kind, is not jealous or boastful, is not arrogant or rude. Love does not insist on its own way, is not irritable or resentful, does not rejoice at wrong but rejoices in the right. Love bears all things, hopes all things, endures all things. (1 *Co* 13:4-7)

Love – and God is love – is the power that protects us and the medicine that heals us from the deadly sins and their consequences. Life, everywhere, is marked by the presence and consequences of these sins, the sins themselves and their offspring. But our struggle is alongside Christ and so we are full of hope, not looking to what has passed but looking to the future and to the prize of the upward call in Christ Jesus.

Conclusion

The monastic teacher Evagrius Pontus spoke of eight 'generic thoughts' in which every thought is contained. These he named as gluttony, fornication, love of money, depression, anger, listlessness, vainglory and pride. These were to become the seven deadly sins of Christian tradition, written about by Chaucer, Dante, John of the Cross, and many others, and still informing popular culture today. Gregory the Great and Thomas Aquinas combine the idea of eight with the tradition of seven by regarding pride as a 'super sin', the root of the other seven.

Evagrius immediately adds this important observation:

> Whether these thoughts come to disturb the soul or not is not something we can control; but whether they linger or not, and whether they arouse passions or not, that is subject to our control.

It is essential to remember this, that we will find these thoughts in us without our having decided to invite them in. Many of the psychological knots in which our thoughts and feelings become entangled arise from these generic thoughts. Once again, such difficulties are not automatically sinful. There are psychological and even physical factors that need to be understood before we can think of making any moral judgement about them.

So how do they become sinful, even deadly or capital sins? It depends on what we do with them and the ways in which we allow them to influence our thinking, our speech and our actions. They are deadly not because they are all necessarily 'mortal' in themselves (Thomas Aquinas, for example, thinks that vainglory is normally a venial sin) but because of the way in which they bind and blind us, desensitising us to the requirements of justice and love. In that sense they are deadly, killing something crucial. They are called capital sins because they are, in Gregory's words, generals that bring armies in their train. They open doors for other vices to enter in.

If the task of Christians, and indeed of humanity generally, is to live together in charity then these are the things to watch out for because these are the most serious enemies of charity. Each of them, as we would expect, is about something good which, properly valued and rightly used, serves to build us up and lead us to maturity. But each of them is about something so fundamental to our sense of ourselves and our way of surviving in the world, that it can become part of our way of saving our life in this world, which, as Jesus tells us, means losing it as far as the kingdom of God is concerned. For example, a proper sense of self-esteem is psychologically and spiritually desirable. If it tends to become pride or if it fails to leave room, as love requires it ought, for self-denial and for sacrifice, then something good is in danger of turning into something bad.

Sin is always a tragedy because it means the corruption of something good. It means that a capacity and energy for action, which could be put at the disposal of virtue, is being directed instead to vicious ends. The contradictory Buddhist proverbs referred to above contain this wisdom: the three conditions under which deeds are produced are covetousness, hatred, and infatuation; the three conditions under which deeds are produced are freedom from covetousness, freedom from hatred, and freedom from infatuation. There is energy in pride, covetousness, lust, anger, gluttony, envy and sloth. To the extent that we are subject to the power of these sins the energy that could be devoted to faith, hope, charity, prudence, justice, temperance and fortitude is squandered. Not only that, such energy is then given to building up the kingdom of this world rather than the kingdom of God. They strengthen falsehood, hatred and injustice, where the virtues would construct the community of truth, love and integrity.

A first step in countering their influence is to understand their psychological and spiritual roots in human experience. This is what this booklet has tried to do. If we stand, humbly, in the truth about ourselves, we will appreciate the power of God's love to heal and strengthen our nature, for love is not jealous or boastful, not arrogant or rude, not irritable or resentful. If we understand the origins and nature in us of these 'generic thoughts', these 'phantasies' or 'demons', we are already in possession of a truth that sets us free. For that understanding assures us, in case we are tempted to doubt it, that our wellbeing and our salvation consists only, and always, in love. This will then sustain us in the discipline and practices of the spiritual life.

Further Reading

Evagrius Pontus, *Praktikos* (translated by John Eudes Bamberger OCSO) Cistercian Publications, Spencer, Massachusetts, 1970

Gregory the Great, *Morals on the Book of Job Parker*, Oxford and Rivington, London, 1850, Book XXXI, 42-45

John Cassian, *The Conferences* (translated by Boniface Ramsey OP) Paulist Press, New York and Mahwah, 1997, Conference V

John of the Cross, *Dark Night of the Soul* (translated by E.Allison Peers) Bantam Doubleday Dell Publishing Group, 1990, Book I, chapters 1-7

McCabe, Herbert, *The Teaching of the Catholic Church,* Darton, Longman and Todd, London, 2000

McCoy, Alban, 'The Seven Deadly Sins', in *An Intelligent Person's Guide to Catholicism,* Continuum, London and New York, 2001, pages 87-115

Sayers, Dorothy, 'The Other Six Deadly Sins', in *Creed or Chaos?* Sophia Institute Press, Manchester NH, 1995, pages 85-113

Spiritual Warfare

Every Christian is engaged in an ongoing struggle against the self, and against temptation, striving to gain the blessings of the Kingdom of God. This booklet enlightens the struggle by searching the wisdom of the scriptures. It gives hope to everyone, because Christ is always by our side to help us in every battle, and he has already defeated death and sin.

ISBN: 978 1 86082 421 0

CTS Code: SP 16

Rediscovering Virtue

In a world where it has become normal for individuals to decide for themselves what is right and what is wrong, the traditional Christian virtues are not often mentioned. However, now more than ever, the sure moral compass provided by justice, religion, prudence, temperance and courage is necessary to live a truly Christian life in faith hope and love.

ISBN: 978 1 86082 454 8

CTS Code: SP 20

The Trinity and the Spiritual Life

The Holy Trinity is a mystery beyond human comprehension but, as this booklet proves, to delve into the mystery of God can bring countless benefits to our relationships with others as well as with God. God is a loving community of persons who invites each one of us to our ultimate goal, to join in the life of the Trinity itself.

ISBN: 978 1 86082 436 4

CTS Code: SP 18

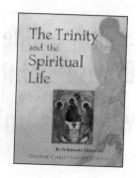